A+ books
Go Go Global

PEOPLE of the WORLD

by Nancy Loewen and Paula Skelley

raintree

a Capstone company — publishers for children

Look in the **mirror.**

United States

Whose **face** do you **see?**

France

You see **you** and

I see **me**.

Every face is special.

China

Nicaragua

Indonesia

Brazil

Every face **belongs**.

Lebanon

Canada

Thailand

Ghana

Our **faces** tell a **story** ...

Madagascar

Jamaica

so say it **loud** and **strong!**

Madagascar

Your eyes
may be
brown.

Philippines

Your eyes may be **blue.**

But **each day**
they **open** to
a **world** that's
new.

India

A **smile** says, "hello".

England

Malaysia

Egypt

Russia

Cuba

Germany

A **smile** says, **"goodbye".**

A smile says, "I love you".

Botswana

United States

A **smile** says,
"I'll try".

17

Vietnam

We use our **hands** to

do, do, **do** ...

to **sew** a
dress

Thailand

Sweden

or **make** a **stew.**

Write

Bolivia

or **play.**

Argentina

Plant

England

or **pray**.

Our
hands
keep **busy**
every day.

India

21

Our **arms** can **throw**.

The Bahamas

Germany

Our **legs** can **run**.

South Africa

Our **feet** can **dance.**

England

Let's have some fun!

24

United States

Thailand

New Zealand

Canada

We start life
small ...

Brazil

Tanzania

United States

then **grow** and **grow.**

China

We **change** the **world** ...

Greece

Vietnam

wherever
we go!

GLOSSARY

mirror smooth, shiny surface that shows the image of the person or thing in front of it

pray speak to God or a god to give thanks or to ask for help

sew make, repair or fasten something with a needle and thread

stew dish made of vegetables and meat or fish cooked together in a liquid

GO GO GLOBAL DISCUSSION QUESTIONS

1. What do all of the people in this book have in common?

2. Name four things in this book that people around the world may do with their hands.

3. Which smiles in this book are most like yours? Which smiles are least like yours? How are they different?

Raintree is an imprint of Capstone Global Library Limited, a company incorporated in England and Wales having its registered office at 7 Pilgrim Street, London, EC4V 6LB – Registered company number: 6695582

www.raintree.co.uk
myorders@raintree.co.uk

Text © Capstone Global Library Limited 2016
The moral rights of the proprietor have been asserted.

Edited by Jill Kalz
Designed by Juliette Peters
Picture research by Tracy Cummins
Production by Tori Abraham
Printed and bound in China.

ISBN 978 1 474 70371 0
19 18 17 16 15
10 9 8 7 6 5 4 3 2 1

British Library Cataloguing in Publication Data
A full catalogue record for this book is available from the British Library.

Acknowledgements
Dreamstime: Alessio Moiola, 26 BL, Konstantin Shevtsov, 14 BL, Sjors737, 20 Top, Woraphon Banchobdi, 25 TR; Getty Images: Asiaselects, 2, Mark D Phillips, 23; iStockphoto: bo1982, 28 Top, Britta Kasholm-Tengve, 26 BR, Casarsa, 20 Bottom, IPGGutenbergUKLtd, 22 Top; Shutterstock: Aleksandar Todorovic, 14 BR, Alliance, 1 TR, Anton_Ivanov, Cover BR, Banana Republic images, 6 BR, berna namoglu, 15, Blend Images, 25 TL, bonga1965, 5 TR, Digital Media Pro, 24, dome, 14 TR, dr322, 8, 10 Top, Filipe Frazao, 5 Bottom, frantab, 17, John Bill, 29, karelnoppe, 1 BM, 14 TL, KOMISAR, 3, leocalvett, Cover, 1 (globe), Lucian Coman, 16, luckypic, 21 Top, mezzotint, 22 Bottom, MidoSemsem, 14 Middle, Monkey Business Images, Cover Back, 1 TL, Natalia Dobryanskaya, 28 Bottom, Naypong, 18, Patryk Kosmider, Cover TL, photoff, Cover TR, Praisaeng, 19 Top, Pressmaster, 1 BR, Rawpixel, 25 Bottom, riekephotos, 6 BL, rj lerich, 5 TL, Ruslan Guzov, 27, Shyamalamuralinath, 21 Bottom, Solis Images, 19 Bottom, spyx, 10 Bottom, stawek, 30 TL , Sura Nualpradid, 7, szefei, 4, 12, testing, Cover BL, uliaLine, 11, ZouZou, 1 BL, Zurijeta, 6 Top; SuperStock: age fotostock, 9, 26 Top.

Every effort has been made to contact copyright holders of material reproduced in this book. Any omissions will be rectified in subsequent printings if notice is given to the publisher.

BOOKS

Families (Our Global Community), Lisa Easterling (Raintree, 2008)

Families Around the World (Around the World), Clare Lewis (Raintree, 2015)

Living Beside a River (Places We Live), Ellen Labrecque (Raintree, 2015)

Population Infographics (Infographics), Chris Oxlade (Raintree, 2014)

WEBSITES

www.bbc.co.uk/schools/barnabybear/
Travel the world with Barnaby Bear.